T0099942

# The Day
# **God**
# Showed Up

# Gordon C. Helsel

WestBow
PRESS
A DIVISION OF THOMAS NELSON

*WestBow Press books may be ordered through booksellers or by contacting:*

*WestBow Press*
*A Division of Thomas Nelson*
*1663 Liberty Drive*
*Bloomington, IN 47403*
*www.westbowpress.com*
*1-(866) 928-1240*

*Cover Photo credit:*

*E. B. Dashiell*
*Poquoson, Virginia*
*www.ebdashiell.smugmug.com*

*ISBN: 978-1-4497-8204-7 (sc)*
*ISBN: 978-1-4497-8205-4 (e)*

*Library of Congress Control Number: 2013902292*

*Printed in the United States of America*

*WestBow Press rev. date: 03/22/2013*

**Art and Mike (Art is on left & Mike is on right)**

This book is dedicated to all the brave men and women who gave their lives for our country and who distinguished themselves while serving in the jungles and rice paddies of Vietnam.

To all who served with Charlie Company, Second Battalion, 35th Infantry, Fourth Infantry Division, I thank you for playing a role in saving my life. And I give thanks to Art and Mike, who gave their lives while trying to protect their fellow soldiers.

Thanks go to all. I will never forget you and the price you paid in service to your country.

I trust that all who read this book will forever remember those who sacrificed their lives for their country.

# Introduction

It's been forty-five years since I left the jungles and rice paddies of Vietnam. I know that many of my comrades don't speak much about their experiences in a combat zone, but I made God a promise many years ago that I would always speak out when given an opportunity. I said I would always tell people about the miracles of February 27, 1968. I guess you could say I struck a deal with God: "Get me out of this place, and I will tell my story."

Well here it is: *The Day God Showed Up.* It isn't intended to be a best seller. It is simply the story I promised God I would tell.

I do not profess to be a great author; however, if what you read in this small book has a positive impact on your life, the time and effort were well worth it. God granted me a miracle forty-five years ago, and He has been continuing those blessings ever since.

I believe, for me, that a song said it best: "I've a roof

up above me, I've a good place to sleep, I've food on my table and shoes on my feet. You gave me your love, Lord, and a fine family. Thank you, Lord, for your blessings on me."

# Chapter 1

## In the Beginning

I pen the words of this book for one reason and one reason only, and that is to share with as many people as I can what God did for me while I was a young soldier in the Republic of Vietnam. I had always heard that God would sometimes show up at the most critical time in our lives, while we were going through some trial or tribulation, and that's what happened to me. God showed up just in the nick of time. A few minutes later, and I would not be sharing my story with you.

I seek only one accomplishment through the words on the pages of this book: that hopefully someone will read what happened to me and know that God has no favorites. You see, what He did for me, He will do for anyone. I am thankful to anyone who acquires this book, and I pray my story will bring you closer to God than you have ever been. I sincerely hope you find *The*

*Day God Showed Up* to be as comforting for you to read as it was for me to write.

I remember that the early days of my life, from about six years of age, were pretty wonderful and uneventful. My family of seven lived near Langley Air Force Base, Virginia, in some converted troop barracks called Langley View. While it is hard to remember being six, I do remember my four sisters and I (and, of course, Mom and Dad) enjoying the environment in which we found ourselves. Time seemed to pass very quickly from my childhood until I became a teenager. It seems as if seven years just disappeared as quickly as the sun sets in the evening.

My teenage years also were relatively uneventful. I did what most teenagers did at eighteen years of age; I went to school and played baseball and football. In retrospect, when my wife, Joy, and I raised our two sons, they mirrored exactly the activities in which I participated (only they were much better at them than I was). School was not really something that held my interest. Oh, I went to school and often barely got by; a D on my report card was actually a "badge of honor." Honestly, I just didn't care.

I think it was my freshman year in high school when

my life started to change. I did not know that when I signed up for an art class, I would meet my future wife. I sat across the table from this beautiful girl, and I confess that I could not have cared less about art. But I cared a *great* deal for the girl across the table! After each art class, there were paint trays that had to be cleaned, dried, and put away. I always made sure I cleaned my pan at the same time that this beautiful girl cleaned hers. From that art class on, my life would never be the same.

Joy and I began to date sometime midyear in the ninth grade. From those days until now, she has always been right by my side, always being the comforter, the friend, and the partner that God ordained long before I joined the world. I always thought that meeting Joy, getting to know her, and eventually loving her were the best days of my life. But there were more blessings to come.

The best day of my life came in September of 1966, a beautiful Saturday afternoon, when we became husband and wife. I was on top of the world. I thought, *It just can't get any better than this.*

Joy and I lived in a small apartment in the same building where she had lived with her mother and sister. We had the best times in that little place, and every time I pass it today, it brings back so many wonderful memories. I mean, how *could* life get any better? A beautiful wife, a 1966 Volkswagen, a roof over our heads—man, this is good stuff!

As a young married couple, the working world called Joy to NASA and me to Newport News Shipbuilding. My job was really okay for a while, even though I was filthy at the end of the day. While I was quite thankful to have a job, I always had this strange feeling that my life was about to change. I could not put my finger on what it meant, and I even tried to dismiss it, but this feeling continued to beat on my conscience. I wondered when, or if, it would ever stop.

# Chapter 2

## Bad News

One afternoon, while at work, I was told I had a phone call in the construction trailer, which was not far from the pit of mud in which I was in up to my knees. I was ready for a break; however, the next five minutes, from the mud hole to the phone inside the trailer, marked a turning point in my life. I picked up the receiver to hear Joy on the other end, and she was crying. That put the fear in my body. Was she sick? Had there been an accident? Was it a family member or what?

She said, "Gordon, you've been drafted!"

"I've been *what?*"

"Drafted, and you have to report to the draft board on a certain day."

I was dumbfounded! All of my dreams, all of the plans I was counting on, faded to black. Gone in a two-minute phone call.

I walked back, zombie-like, to finish making my mud hole larger, trying to reason and understand in my mind how all of a sudden my country needed me. I wondered, *Why me? Aren't there plenty of single guys they could take?*

What a selfish thing to think. I could feel the blood rise from my feet to my head. *Now here I am, part of a young couple, married six months, happy and enjoying life. How can they do this to me? I will fight it,* I decided, and I began to think of ways to get out of my situation.

Joy and I did the best we could over the next couple of weeks, until I unexpectedly received another notice from the draft board. I was actually afraid to open the letter, but I thought, *These people have already ruined my life. What in the world could they possibly do to make things worse?* As I slowly opened the envelope and pulled the letter from the envelope, I could not believe what I was reading. I was not drafted. *Wow!* Apparently, my country did not need my services after all, and I totally agreed.

*Man, I can't wait to get back into my mud pit tomorrow!* I was right back up on top of the mountain. However, I still needed to continue my fight to do something to keep from being drafted in the future. I told my wife, "I will join the national guard, or maybe the navy reserves. I think I will touch base with the marine reserves. Maybe they will take me." I concluded that six months of active duty and then one weekend a month surely beat two years away from home, not to mention God knows where!

Speaking of God, I never gave Him a thought after that second letter came. I just told people I was lucky and let it go at that. I wish I could say that I stayed on the mountain of happiness, but that was not to be. I had spoken with every reserve unit I possibly could. I just hadn't thought about all the thousands of guys just like me who had the same idea. The answer from the national guard and the navy were the same: no room for one more person—not one! Then the marine reserves came through. "We will take you," a recruiter told me. "Prepare for some medical testing, and off you go."

I should have known that any good news I received now would not last, and it didn't. The very next day, another letter from the draft board came. My country needed me again. I simply could not believe it. I phoned the draft board to explain that I was joining the marine reserves, and while I appreciated their concern for me, I believed the marines needed one more good man.

After speaking with the draft board and explaining my position, I had this tickle in my stomach. I thought the draft board had tried to ruin my life, and I fought back. I dodged a bullet—no pun intended!

Joy and I spent a few weeks anxiously awaiting any information from the marine reserves. I allowed myself to fantasize about how sharp I would look in the dress blues of a US marine. I even thought Joy would be impressed. There is just something about a marine in dress blues, you know? The roller coaster continued. After the next week, I had decided how things would be. Then another letter from the draft board arrived. "You will not be joining the marine reserves. The draft board supersedes the reserves. We got you first. You will be a soldier in the US Army, and you will spend at least two years (and maybe more) in the army." No Marine Corps, no dress blues, right back to the valley of depression, crushed again. I tried to blame anyone I could, including God. I made up my mind and truly believed that God was responsible for crushing my dreams, and I could not understand why He would allow my life to be tossed around like a small boat in a storm. "Why, God?" I asked. There was no answer, and that was fine with me. Then days later, the time had run out. Reality was about to set in, and there was absolutely nothing I could do to stop what I figured would be the very worst day of my life. But I was to realize later that something of a greater magnitude was just around the corner.

# Chapter 3

## Army Basic and Advanced Training

As I said good-bye to Joy and boarded the bus to basic training, I fought back the tears and tried to ignore the ache in my stomach. Next stop: Fort Bragg, North Carolina. After what felt like an eternity, the bus pulled into Fort Bragg. As we stepped off the bus, our welcoming party consisted of eight of the largest men I had ever seen, and man were they mad! These guys started yelling, cussing, and calling us names of every description—and we had just arrived! How would I bear eight weeks of this? I never thought I would make it.

Once I was in the routine, things became a little bit better; not that much, but a little. The eight weeks finally drew to a close. We were close to graduation from basic training, and I couldn't wait to see Joy. I had missed her terribly and thought, hopefully, that being with her just a couple of hours would somehow give me the strength to move on to advanced training. About three hours after graduation, and after saying good-bye to Joy, my mom and dad, and my sister Judy, there was another bus, another long ride, another eight weeks of training, and I would be done. I remembered that the army had asked me, "Son, what would you like to do for your two years in the army, and where would you like to be stationed?" Actually, I had thought that was very thoughtful, and I had answered, "I would like to be a military policeman, and Fort Monroe would be a great fit for me, since my home is only twenty minutes away from the Fort." Just eight more weeks and then a gravy train for the rest of my tour.

We pulled into Fort Jackson, South Carolina, at approximately 2 a.m. on a Thursday, and when we arrived, our reactions were actually quite subdued; I was surprised. After everyone was off the bus, we were told to fall in, to shut our mouths, and to listen very, very carefully. What I heard next buckled my knees. The drill sergeant very calmly said, "Listen up, men. Let me be clear. After your eight weeks here at Fort Jackson, each and every one of you will be assigned to an infantry unit in Vietnam. Get that in your head right now. You are *all* going to Vietnam." I broke into a cold sweat. Surely

I had misunderstood the sergeant. I pushed my buddy and asked him, "What did he say?"

"He said we are all going to Vietnam."

"Wait a minute. They told me I would be a military policeman. I am supposed to be stationed at Fort Monroe. Why would the army change its mind?" Both my mind and heart were racing! I had to talk to Joy. Somehow, she would have some comforting words. I was still in shock, standing straight up, thinking, *I'm going to war. I'm bound for a land ten thousand miles from home, to have someone try to kill me every day for a year, and I will probably have to kill as well.* Later, I finally reached Joy on the phone. I believe she was as shocked as I was, but somehow she was composed and helped calm me down. I remember thinking as I starred at the ceiling of my barracks, *Dear God, what are you doing? How much more can you put on me? God, I don't want to kill people, and I surely don't want to be killed.* I had decided that God had abandoned me, and you know what? I just didn't care.

Advanced training went well, and I learned very quickly what my specialty would be; 11 Bravo, it was called. In other words, my specialty would be to carry an M-16, six hand grenades, and a pack with 75 pounds of stuff on my back. I am nineteen years old, and I am going to war. And I will die in that war. I will come home in a casket covered with the colors of my country, and that was it. Only a few months after my funeral, I would be forgotten by everyone except my family.

# Chapter 4

## Going to 'Nam

The day that I left for Vietnam is burned into my mind and heart. The trip to the airport and the thoughts of leaving Joy behind made me sick. The trip to the airport was painful; it was just a few miles closer to Vietnam. *I have got to be strong,* I thought. *How can I be?* I hugged my wife and fought back tears as I walked to the plane. And as I took my seat by the window, I could still see Joy waving and crying. *I wish this plane would move. I can't stand this.* Finally, the plane did move, and slowly, I lost sight of Joy. I closed my eyes and waited for the takeoff.

The flight to Oakland, California, was incredibly long, but finally, we arrived. All I could think was, *I am five hours closer to Vietnam.* We were on the ground in Oakland for just a few hours. I was once again airborne. Next stop: Cam Ranh Bay, South Vietnam.

# Chapter 5

## Arriving in Vietnam

Seven hours later, the landscape of Vietnam came into view. From thirty thousand feet, you could see rice paddies and the mountains; they all looked so beautiful. Then suddenly the wheels of the plane touched the runway. I was here, about to become part of the reality I had dreaded for months. When the plane came to a stop at the gate, I gathered my personal belongings and walked off the plane. We were met by fellow army personnel and bussed to a hangar, where we would be issued the essentials for combat. After receiving my M-16 rifle, green underwear, green fatigues, and a rucksack designed to carry a lot of weight, we hopped on a Huey helicopter bound for the unit where I would be assigned. About forty minutes out, the chopper began to circle a large mountain that had all the vegetation at the top removed. I could see the bunkers and a few soldiers scurrying around. This was it. I would shortly be walking in a combat zone. How did this happen? I still couldn't believe I was there.

The chopper landed gently on top of this mountain, and I was led by a young sergeant E-5, who was assigned to get me squared away. We walked together to a bunker complex. For some reason I thought, *Hey, this might not be so bad. These bunkers are fortified with sandbags, M-60 machine guns pointed to the east, and army cots for sleeping. Wow! Not bad at all. They even have a shower tent.*

As I began to unpack, the same sergeant E-5 walked into the bunker. "Private," he said, "this is not your unit. There has been a mistake." He then asked me to follow him, and I did. We walked a few feet and peered over the edge of the mountain. "See those men about two hundred yards away? That's your unit. Charlie Company, Second Battalion, 35th Infantry."

As I said good-bye to my new friend in arms, I started down the side of the hill, my new jungle boots sinking in the mud. I was stumbling as each step brought me closer to the unit, closer to some of the men who would later come home in a casket with the colors of their country draping the metal box. With each step, the mud got deeper. It was orange mud, and it clung to everything. I finally reached my unit, and the guys seemed sincere when they shook my hand and said, "Welcome to the 'Nam." No matter what, I was here and ready to serve my country.

# Chapter 6

## My First Patrol

I remember the unbearable heat. I just needed to rest a minute. For some reason, I believed that I would get some sleep soon. However, that was not to be. I was assigned to the second platoon, which was moving out on patrol right then! I guess I shouldn't have been surprised. So far, everything I had thought war was about had proven to be wrong. The platoon moved out, with this rookie troop without a clue of what to do right in the middle of a group of seasoned soldiers. As we moved away from the landing zone, I kept looking back and thinking, *Will I ever see this landing zone again? Will I step on some booby trap and lose my legs or arms? Will I find myself in a position to take another person's life?* My mind was so full of negative thoughts, it was just a blur.

I was frightened for sure, but there was nothing but

jungle, mud, and dampness, and, of course, the ever-present leeches. I must have looked zombie-like as we moved toward an unknown objective. Finally came a time to rest, take a quick drink of water, and offload some of this weight from my back. Almost as soon as my canteen was back in its holder, someone shouted, "Saddle up," which means (I found out later), "Put your pack on your back, grab your weapon, and keep moving."

*What's wrong with these people?* I wondered. *We will all die from exhaustion if we don't get some rest.* Finally, after what seemed like a lifetime, we did stop.

"How long will this rest break be?" I asked the guy behind me.

"Not long," was his reply. "We've got ambush tonight."

"Ambush? What in the world is ambush?"

As the sun began to set and darkness drew ever closer, I learned all about what ambush meant. We moved out shortly before daylight was gone. The platoon leader located a trail that looked well traveled. Great. *Great place for an ambush*, I thought. We all found places to sit and placed claymore mines out in front of us. We locked and loaded our weapons. If anyone passed in front of us, he would surely die. As I sat behind a bush, super observant, I thought, *What if a child passes by ... or a group of Vietnamese women invade our ambush?* I didn't want to think about it. I couldn't think about it. I just wanted the night to end, and finally it did. No one had passed on our trail that night, but that would change.

We set many ambushes, and many Vietnamese found themselves in what they must have thought was the end of the world. For many, it was. We used claymore mines, M-16 rifles, M-60 machine guns, and hand grenades—none of which had a conscience. They didn't care whose lives they took, the enemy's or ours. After my first ambush and patrol, I started to think I was a seasoned veteran, that now I was somehow a combat hardened soldier. Not so! I was about to be educated by war. Not a day passed that I did not witness some sort of death, whether that be a Vietcong soldier or one of our own.

The sight of a young soldier, not older than me, who had his life ended in a rice paddy, thousands of miles from home. I wondered, *Was he married? Did he have kids? Were his parents waiting patiently for their son's return home?* All I could do was think and help carry his body to a chopper, starting his long ride home.

Over the weeks and months, everything ran together.

I got used to being filthy and wet. I got accustomed to the smell of death, patrolling, and setting ambushes. Would this journey ever be over? Every day brought the same activities: patrol, dig a hole, and maybe sleep an hour while your buddy covered you. As days turned into weeks, and weeks into months, I began to think, *Maybe I will make it. Maybe I will get home to Joy safely, and we can live happily ever after, putting this horror behind us.* But that was not to be. Little did I know in just a few days, my life would change forever.

Charlie Company had been given an objective to seize somewhere north of the city of Da Nang. By this time, I had been promoted and was now a team leader, responsible for a few guys. I took it seriously. I put my life in their hands, and they had put their lives in mine. *Together—somehow—we will all make it,* I thought. There was a never-ending bond that lasts to this day. It was a Friday morning, as I recall, when we moved toward our objective. We had just cleared the jungle and were approaching a small river. My team was assigned the point, meaning out in front of the company. I drew the short straw, so there I was, walking point. As we approached the river, I thought I saw movement, but many things seem to move when you walk point. We moved closer to the river's edge, and there, ten yards in front of me, were four heavily armed Vietnamese soldiers.

It appeared they were looking across the river for some reason. As we crept closer, my left thumb slowly moved the switch on my M-16 from single shot to automatic. Still, they had not heard us. One more step, I pulled the trigger, they all fell to the ground. I stopped to reload, while the rest of the team finished the job. We moved ever so slowly to the bodies of those now-dead soldiers. Except for one, who had somehow tried to hide himself in the brush. One more bullet did the job, and he stopped moving.

The practice after an incident, like the one we had just been through, was to search the bodies for maps, weapons, or anything else of use. The young man in the brush was mine to search. The young soldier was faceup on the ground. He was probably older than me, and probably did not want to be where he was any more than I did. Suddenly as I picked up his helmet, I saw there in the top a picture of a beautiful, young Vietnamese woman. My stomach turned as I thought about how I had taken his life. Was this his wife? His daughter? His sister? My mind drifted to my wife, Joy, and I was just sick. I had to compose myself though. If the tables were turned, no doubt he would have killed me. Funny how that statement kind of jump-starts your system. I placed the young man's helmet beside him, with the picture where it was, and I left him there. I sincerely hoped other Vietnamese soldiers would find his body and send him home to his beautiful woman. Though somehow you begin to accept causing the death of another human being, I still see their faces today. However, killing is not an ego booster; you just learn to cope with it.

# Chapter 7

## Another Tragedy

During war, it is hard to believe how many tragedies occur that have nothing to do with facing the enemy. Many times during my tour in Vietnam, men were severely injured while actually resting from combat and their long patrols through the jungles and rice paddies of Vietnam. I recall a late afternoon after our squad leader had met with the company commander. They returned to the area, where we were just lying back, resting. This particular squad leader was known to me only as "Red." Red returned to brief the rest of us regarding the next day's patrol. In his arms was the customary case of beer and soda mix—my preference were the grape drinks. Red stepped over me to drop the case of beer and soda on the ground. When he dropped the case, the resulting explosion nearly caused my eardrums to burst. After the smoke cleared and I regained my senses, there was Red, in total agony.

The night before, we had set our visual ambush. As day began to draw near, we prepared to collect the claymore mines that we had set the evening before. Claymore mines, you will remember, were an instrument of total debilitation and death. The mines were simple, actually, but so deadly. The mines were attached to a blasting cap and set at the edge of a trail. The mine itself was just ball bearings embedded in a core of C-4 explosive. The detonation happened with the press of a handheld device that sent a pulse of electrical current to the blasting cap, resulting in the explosion. That is what sent the ball bearings flying toward their target.

Red had not disconnected the electrical device from the mine, so when he dropped the case of beer and soda, the weight was enough to trigger the electrical device of the mine, and it exploded. I can still hear the cries for a medic and see the sight of Red's right leg gone. This was not supposed to happen! Red was a good man, a very knowledgeable man, the kind of man who always leads. Just another incident of war, another injury on the list, another evacuation, but Red's life was changed forever.

## The Day God Showed Up

I looked toward the cloudless sky and silently asked God, *Why? Why Red? Why are we here? Why are we out every day, trying to kill as many of the enemy as we can? In the end, what have we really accomplished?* The questions kept coming. Was it worth the fifty thousand plus who died in that far-off country? Was it worth the countless veterans still extremely scarred by the war? I pray for them and for their families each day. I ask that now, as you read this book, you stop and pray for those who fought for all Americans. I am proud to have served with such exceptional soldiers.

This may sound extremely strange to you, but I feel that I was blessed to have had those experiences. What I know now is that God knew precisely how these experiences would change both my life and my outlook. In Vietnam, I found myself checking off the days. I would notch my M-16 at the end of each day, and I could not wait to be able to count 365 notches. But as with other things of war about which I had been wrong, so it was with this.

# Chapter 8

## On-the-Job Training

I recall the company commander, Lieutenant Kraut, called me to his location one evening. I thought, *Man, what could I have done to warrant a visit to the CO?* Lieutenant Kraut was a born leader, a concerned leader, and I felt comfortable following him. When I got to his location, the visit was short and to the point. "Helsel," he said, "you are now the company explosives expert. Take this time to fuse all the C-4 you can carry, and don't forget the blasting caps." I was stunned, thinking, *I'm no expert in blowing things up! Man, why me?* If I had impressed Lieutenant Kraut in some way, I wished I had not. Explosives expert. I just grinned as I saluted and returned to my platoon.

The next morning, after filling the holes that we had dug the night before, we moved out for another day, wondering as usual if it would be our last. Not far into the patrol, the point man came upon a 250 pound bomb that had not exploded. Lieutenant Kraut guided the platoon away from the bomb, fearing it was booby-trapped. Certainly, if it had exploded, it would have killed us all. As we moved around the bomb, we all got a look at it, just lying there on the ground. We were at least one hundred yards beyond the bomb when I heard my name called. "Helsel, the CO wants you." *Great, I've impressed him again,* I thought. *What's my next new responsibility going to be?*

As I approached Lieutenant Kraut, he said, "Helsel, we will wait here. Go back and blow the bomb up in place."

I thought the company commander had lost his mind. "Blow it in place, sir?" I replied.

"Get on it," he ordered.

"Yes, sir."

As I walked back to the location of the device, every nerve in my body was tingling. In a few minutes, I reached the bomb. The company was out of sight, and I was scared to death. I reached into my new explosives bag and took out one stick of C-4 explosive. I carefully removed a blasting cap and pushed it slowly into the C-4. I then inserted the blasting cap into the time fuse.

With shaking hands, I slowly placed the stick of C-4 onto the bomb. I gently retrieved my bag and walked away from the bomb. As I retreated, I laid several yards of time fuse until I felt that I was far enough away from the bomb. I reached for my matches, lit one, and placed it near the fuse. As the fuse began to burn, I turned and ran as fast as I could to reconnect with my platoon, and waited anxiously with them. A few minutes went by ... no explosion. "I've done something wrong."

Lieutenant Kraut appeared. "Helsel, how much time fuse did you use?"

"It was pretty short, sir," I replied. *He's going to send me back to the bomb,* I thought. *Dear Lord, please let that bomb explode.* It never did. I thought about that day many times over the years and why my first attempt to blow up something failed. Lieutenant Kraut felt we needed to move out, and I agreed with him. I continued to look back, expecting the familiar sound of an explosion any minute. While I later had chances to blow up things, I never became the expert that Lieutenant Kraut had titled me.

I was so happy to see night come. I was totally worn out from fright with my experience with the bomb. I did not expect the very next day to bring yet another test of my ability to use explosives, but during the next day's patrol, about midday, Charlie Company stumbled upon a major tunnel complex. Truly, it made us uneasy to think that somewhere in those tunnels, the enemy was lying in wait. The only way to find out, though, was to enter the tunnels. The first tunnel was very tight for the four of us who entered, with barely room for a small man and his .45 caliber pistol. As we eased our way further into the earth, the tunnel suddenly became higher and wider, and we were able to stand.

The tunnel system was humongous; I have never seen anything like it. We continued to explore the tunnel complex and entered a large room carved into the earth. The room was dark except for the flashlights we carried. The place was musty and had a strange odor. This large room was now, or at some point, had been a hospital carved out of the earth. There were beds and bandages. It was apparent we had made a big find.

Our journey was uneventful with regard to the enemy, but we could not allow the tunnel complex to exist. I stood by, awaiting orders on what to do with the tunnel complex. The word came down; fill the tunnel with explosives and try to destroy it or at least close it off. Soon the sound of a helicopter could be heard circling over our position. The pilot gently settled the chopper on the ground. It was loaded down with cases of hand grenades. We unloaded the hand grenades, and I began to drag them into the tunnels. After placing the boxes in several strategic locations, the so-called expert in explosives (that would be me) was called to set the charge. This time, I must have done it right, because the ground rumbled beneath our feet. After the smoke had settled, I looked at Lieutenant Kraut. He just smiled and said, "Saddle up, and move out."

*What next?* I wondered. *Another day, another notch on my rifle.*

# Chapter 9

## My First Christmas—
## What a Present

Suddenly, it was Christmas in Vietnam! I had a small Christmas tree decorated with tiny balls and some tinsel. Christmas Day was very uneventful, but we did get a hot meal that day—a welcome change. I can still see the helicopter hovering a few feet off the ground and the door gunner tossing our Christmas dinner out the door of the helicopter. The chopper could not take a lot of time hovering. After all, we were still in the enemy's backyard. The fact that it was Christmas meant nothing in war. At any moment, we could be under attack. Something that would be proven later that night.

Just before the sun began going down, we started our daily ritual of digging a hole to retreat into should we be attacked. Hole finished, sandbags in place. Ready now for what may come next. Stretched out in my hole, I had some visitors from the hole next to me. It had been a pretty good day—no patrol, no ambush—just smoking cigarettes, drinking soda, and talking about home. My neighbors had just left me to crawl into their hole when the first artillery round hit.

This could not be happening! No Vietnamese artillery could possibly harm us, not where we were located. Just then, we heard the second round coming, and I was suddenly thanking God for this hole in which I was safe. The round landed directly in our command post. I scrambled out of the safety of my freshly dug hole and headed for the command post. "They're gone." Of the five "killed in actions" lying there in the blood, with the smell of smoke and the shrapnel, I did not recognize a single one of them. All I could do was cry. "Christmas night and these men are dead." Christmas night! The night's event haunted me for several weeks. Five more Americans dead, this time in our own artillery base and by our own artillery round. How could this happen? Christmas night passed into daylight, and only then could we carry our friends, the same friends we had just eaten Christmas dinner with, to a helicopter. They began their final journey home. What could be worse than knowing your son, husband, or brother was killed Christmas night? It would ruin Christmas for all those families for every year to come. This was just another day of death and destruction, with death, again, getting the upper hand.

# Chapter 10

## Air Support with a Twist

I was up early the next day. For some reason, I just couldn't rest. Strange how you can get used to no sleep or sleeping in three inches of water. Moving out of our night location, we were ordered on a search and destroy mission. The title itself tells the purpose.

As we approached the village, small-arms fire pinned us down in a rice paddy. We needed some air power, and we needed it now! First came the helicopter gunships. Man, what a job they did! Next came the jets, pounding the village from the air. All we could so was lie in the rice paddies and wait for the planes to finish their work.

Just when I thought the jets were finished, one of them banked left and was coming right for us. The pilot had mistaken us for enemy soldiers and was determined to finish the job. I watched in fear as the pilot fired his missiles. It looked as though a thousand needles were coming at us. The missile hit behind our position, and the jet headed for his base. Talk about a close call; those missiles certainly would have killed the entire company. It may sound funny, but I'm so glad he missed!

Finally, we moved out into the village. What I expected was there—the smell of gunfire and dead bodies. We searched the village thoroughly and then left, leaving dead men, women, and children, casualties of the gunships and jets. *This war! Even small children are now being killed and wounded. It's got to stop!* Wishful thinking. What I thought and what would be were two completely different scenarios. I wished I could put an end to this travesty now and forever.

Fast forward to February 26, 1968. In consultation with the brigade commander, my company commander had decided to rest the company for the majority of the day. While that was extremely unusual, the thought of having a whole day and night to rest and write letters home was certainly a welcome thought. However, in battle the end of a day can ruin the good news heard earlier.

At about 6:00 p.m., Lieutenant Kraut summoned all the squad leaders and team leaders to the company command post to brief us on the mission for the next day. Listening to him spell out the mission, we knew we were in for a fight. He told us that we would helicopter to the base of a mountain several miles away. After leaving the helicopters, we would begin to ascend the mountain until the summit was reached. You can only imagine how I felt when I learned that from the base of the mountain to its peak, there were elements of the North Vietnamese Second Division dug in and well armed. As I thought about the mission, I tried to predetermine what I would do, how I would react should we engage the enemy. I was troubled by the sheer numbers. Our company existed of about fifty troops. A division of the North Vietnamese Regulars would be hundreds. I did not sleep at all that night. All I could think about was the mission and on the feeling that I and many others would die the next day. Still wanting to control my future, I tried to decide how I wanted my life to end, but to no avail; no answers surfaced. I was scared and nervous knowing we needed more men and more ammo, and we needed God Himself to lead this company. I even prayed the twenty-seventh of February would never come. It was a foolish thought, since the earth would have to stop spinning in order for that to happen. But God had parted the Red Sea for the Israelites, why not have a few less revolutions?

Yet again, my plans were thwarted. Shortly after sunrise on the February 27, you could hear several helicopters in the distance. *Here comes our ride to hell,* was my thought. The helicopters circled a couple of times before easing to the ground. We boarded the helicopter, just as we had many times before; however, the mood was so different. No joking, no conversation. We just glanced at one another, wondering who would live and who would die. Our flight ended. We jumped from the helicopters and ran for the closest cover we could find. Everyone looked toward the mountain, awaiting the order to move out. Finally, the order came, and we moved out. We all carried more ammo than normal and clipped extra grenades to our belts. We moved slowly on a well-traveled trail, cautiously expecting contact at any time. We encountered areas of thick bamboo, where the only way through was to use our machetes to clear a path.

Soon we cleared the bamboo and reached the trail again. We rested a few minutes after clearing the bamboo. A drink of water, a check of my M-16, and we were off again, forward and upward, soaking wet with sweat! I thought, *So far so good.*

Another hour on the trail, and we had moved fewer

than one hunded yards. We stopped, and Lieutenant Kraut moved some of the company to the jungles on the left and the right. I was glad I stayed on the trail. As we moved, I just knew we would make contact with the enemy any minute now. Suddenly, there was an explosion, and we all hugged the ground. In war, you have two friends: your comrades and the ground. Now we sought the latter as we waited for word concerning the explosion. Two men killed in action by a booby trap. Two more soldiers dead. Two more families don't know yet that their loved one was killed. We backed down the mountain and watched as two more fallen soldiers were carried to a helicopter. *Man, I hate this place. I won't make it through the day,* I thought.

We continued our quest. Everyone was now repositioned back on the trail, hoping, I guess, for a safer trip to the summit of the mountains. A few hours later, we slowly approached the summit. We were once again told to take a break, an order with which we were more than glad to comply.

When we began our ascent up the mountain, I was walking point, meaning the first person in the column, kind of like a guinea pig. I carried a 12-gauge shotgun, which was customary for a point man. With every step, every leaf that crackled under my feet, every vine I moved with the barrel of my shotgun, I was expecting the enemy to attack. One last rest before the summit. As I pulled my canteen from its holder, a young man named Mike came to my side. He was very new to the company, about two months. "Gordon," he said, "Let me walk point." He felt he was ready. He continued to ask, and I finally agreed as I had walked point for him the day before. Little did I know God had intervened at that very moment. Another miracle for me at the expense of a brave soldier and friend. I handed nineteen-year-old Mike the shotgun, and I fell in behind him. To my rear was a young man named Art, who joined the company at the same time as Mike. He was a friendly guy and so very proud of his two young daughters. He carried an 8 × 10 photo in his rucksack and just beamed whenever he showed it to someone. Art was a giant of a man; a gentle giant would describe him best.

Our course was nearing an end. Mike had been on point about thirty minutes when it happened. In the twinkling of an eye, we were in the fiercest firefight that I had been involved in since arriving in Vietnam. When the first shot rang out, we all hit the ground. We realized that the enemy had formed an ambush in the form of a horseshoe. We were surrounded! *This is it,* I thought. *I'll be dead soon.* There was no way out. We were pinned down and outnumbered. *What do we do?* I thought. I did not know that answer.

The North Vietnamese had launched a devastating amount of fire. The sound of AK-47s and mortars was so powerful and close. *This is the big one,* I thought. The enemy was so close we could hear them talking. I knew at any moment we would be fighting hand to hand. *Where are these guys?* I thought. They were well dug in. Mike, just a few yards ahead of me, rolled onto his stomach and looked back at me, as if to ask what to do. The instant our eyes met, his face turned ashen. Mike did not move again, and I knew he was gone. My mind raced backward; I should have been there, where he was! Why did I allow him to be on point? Nineteen years old going home in a gray box covered with the flag of his country. Art, just inches from me, asked, "What do we do?"

I asked, "Where is the fire coming from? That's where we need to be." He motioned to our right, and we moved together up the embankment. We continued to slowly crawl, firing all the while. Art and I were side by side when he stopped crawling. I knew he was gone as well.

A bullet through his neck had claimed the life of this husband and father of two girls. Art, this giant of a man, now became my protection. I used his body for cover. Art played a major role in saving my life. As I lay nearly completely under Art's body, I fired clip after clip after clip toward the enemy position. Nothing I did was causing them to slow up. *When will the bullet hit me?* I wondered. *How much longer will I be alive? What's it like to die?* I continued to wonder all these thoughts. Mike was dead; Art was dead. I was all by myself, cut off from the main column.

Two hours later, the fire seemed to slow somewhat, and I could hear yelling. At first, I thought the voices were the enemy, but it was Lieutenant Kraut, who had seen my position. He was waving his hands, encouraging me to come to his position. I thought for a few minutes and then decided to run. I would shed all my equipment and run while firing to my left. I had no choice. I began to run. Only a few feet into it, a bullet struck me in the left side, just under my heart, knocking me off my feet. I felt my side; I was bleeding. "I'm alive," I told myself. "I'll try again." I managed to stand and stumbled toward Lieutenant Kraut's position, still firing to my left. A few more steps, and a bullet tore through my left forearm. I fell to the jungle floor, unable to move. The blood from a severed artery began to soak into the dirt. *It is all over for me,* I thought. *I will bleed to death right here.* The voices kept calling, helping me to stay conscious. I began to crawl. With every inch, the blood pumped from my body. I rolled onto my stomach, looking for anyone, but my sight was blurry from lack of blood.

I tried as hard as I could to move forward, but I just couldn't do it. So I lifted my head up to God, and that's when He showed up. Every soldier carried on his rucksack a small bandage wrapped in foil. My rucksack was left behind, so I had no bandage. Others were dead, and Lieutenant Kraut was yards away. As I focused my eyes on something right in front of me, I realized it was a bandage out of the foil, completely opened. I summoned the strength to grab that bandage and place it in the hole in my arm. I prayed to God that it would stop the bleeding. How did that bandage get there, open and ready to apply to my wound? God showed up and placed it there just for me—exactly what I needed, exactly when I needed it.

Again I tried to push forward. I could only use my feet an inch at a time. I was worn out. I remember thinking, *I just can't make it.* The firefight was still in high gear. I could still hear the whiz of bullets over my head and all around me. I remember thinking I might just make it now, as I wasn't losing as much blood after applying the bandage in my wound. I thought maybe someone would come to help and carry me to safety. Suddenly, two feet in front of me, I saw an enemy hand grenade. The enemy was now rolling hand grenades down the embankment and right toward me. I lowered my head and waited for the end. I saw the grenades, I heard the muffled explosions, and I felt the earth around me rumble. I was still alive. No shrapnel, not one piece struck my body. More grenades came, and it was as if there was an invisible circle of armor around me, protecting me. *I've got to move. I've got to move,* I thought. The ordeal had lasted a couple of hours, and I needed to get to safety. *I'm almost there. God has given me the strength to crawl to safety. He has given me the bandage to stop my bleeding, and He has surrounded me with angels to protect me from the hand grenades. I have to go!*

As I finally reached a safe area, I looked up into the eyes of the company's first sergeant. I struggled to speak. Weakly, I asked for a medic. He did not respond. Again I cried out, "I need a medic." It was then I realized he was "frozen" from fright. He simply could not respond.

## The Day God Showed Up

Now out of the field of fire, I remember a friend, Fred Ostendorf, pulling me to complete safety. Then my friend Rocky picked me up and ran with me in his arms to a landing zone the others had cut with machetes. I can remember Fred reciting the Twenty-Third Psalm to me as we raced to the Medivac chopper. I don't have the words to describe the feeling I had when I saw the helicopter with that big white cross on its nose. Once loaded into the Medivac helicopter, I felt it slowly lift off the ground

# Chapter 11

## The Long Road to Recovery

As I looked up into the cloudless sky, I knew God had been with me. He stood between me and the bullets that would have taken my life. He shielded me from those hand grenade explosions, and He placed that bandage at my fingertips. I suppose you would have to have been there and witnessed the miraculous events that happened that day to understand fully the magnitude of it all. Yes, God showed up and, for some reason, spared my life. Maybe it was for no other reason than to pen these words after forty-four years. The helicopter finally arrived at a field hospital, where doctors discussed the removal of my left arm. Being left-handed, I remember thinking, *No, God, not my left hand and arm! Please, God, could you intervene just one more time?*

When I awoke from the first of what would be several operations, my left arm was still there. God intervened again, and I was left wondering, *Why did you save me, Lord? Why didn't I finish walking point that day? Why was Art's body there to protect me? I should be dead. I should have been sent home covered with a US flag.* I vividly remember leaving the field hospital en route to the Philippines and Clark Air Force Base on a C-141 carrying wounded soldiers; I'm not sure how many. I remember my pain, as well as the pain of those who were near death. I knew enough to appreciate the pain medication that finally brought sleep. Even though the sleep didn't last long, it was blessedly painless. I wish I could personally thank all the crew on that big C-141 aircraft. They were so caring, kind, and dedicated to saving as many lives as they could.

How long the road trip lasted I will never know. Sometime during the night, the plane touched down, and as the plane hit the runway, the groans of the wounded were audible. Even with the pilot applying the brakes as gently as he could, any movement of the plane caused unbearable pain. As the medics and others started to transfer us from the plane to a bus located just a short distance from the aircraft, I could see more clearly the soldiers who were wounded beyond belief. There were bullet wounds, shrapnel wounds, and men with one or more limbs missing. There were some men burned beyond recognition. Each one had given so much for their country. I began to cry and to thank God that I was not as seriously disabled as so many were.

The stretcher that I had been lying on for so long was lifted ever so gently by the medics and placed on the bus. We were soon on a short trip to the hospital, where my journey ended on the fifth floor. Going to the fifth floor was not a good thing. I found out later that about 70 percent of those taken there succumbed to their wounds. Commonplace with so many young men and women badly hurt and debilitated, the screams of agony and pain on that floor were deafening. Some died from burns, traumatic brain injury, and from other injuries so serious that no medicine would ever be able to help them. Like the others forever etched in my mind, they went home. These men and women once had the same dreams I had. They looked forward to being reunited with their families and moving forward with the plans they had put on hold to bravely serve their county with pride. I cannot imagine the shock and devastation when wives, husbands, mothers, and fathers heard the news of their soldier's death. It has been said that time heals all wounds. I am not so sure I believe that. There are still millions in pain and discomfort, and I believe they will be forever.

My stay in the Philippines lasted sixteen weeks. Every day more wounded and scared soldiers flowed into the hospital with those same injuries and disfigurement to their bodies. Every day at least one soldier took his or her final breath, surrendering to the injuries.

Over time, even in a hospital, you can experience relationships. Some involve no conversation; just a smile from the doorway of a hospital room brings connections. I recall one young man who had been standing beside a fuel tank when it was struck. He was burned so badly that he was terribly disfigured and spent days in constant agony. I remember looking into his room, trying to understand why. Tubes, lines, and bandages engulfed his entire body. *How long can he stand this ordeal,* I wondered. A few weeks later, I revisited his room, but he had gone home. As I turned around and wheeled back to my room, my temporary home, my thoughts drifted to his family. I prayed that God would comfort them through the grief and tears of their loss.

I sat at my hospital room window, looking into a beautiful blue sky and thinking of those I had left behind in the rice paddies and jungles. Were they all right? Were they safe? Had some returned home safely? I prayed so.

Slow improvement over several weeks led to me being on my way to Hawaii for more surgery and recovery. Twelve weeks in all and more crises to get behind me. I contracted malaria. My fever reached 107. I had alcohol baths every hour on the hour and slept on an air-conditioned mattress for several days. When my fever finally broke, I felt as if I had been hit by a truck. All I had to do then was to rest and recuperate. Unfortunately, a few weeks later, prior to being transferred to Tripler Army Hospital in Hawaii, I had malaria again! I couldn't believe it. Six more weeks in quarantine. *Will I ever get home?* After six weeks, blood tests showed no malaria, however I wasn't out of the woods yet. I experienced an excruciating pain in my chest as the nurse was flushing my IV. This was confirmed by my doctor as a blood clot that had passed thru my heart. Just another miracle from God. Finally, I boarded a C-141 aircraft for the flight to Hawaii. Arriving in Hawaii, all I could think of was Joy and home. *Week by week, I'm getting closer!* A month later came the best new I had ever heard: I was going home! Next stop: Andrews Air Force Base, outside Washington

DC. From there to DeWitt Army Hospital, and finally, Joy will return to my life.

# Chapter 12

## Back to the USA

T he flight from Hawaii to the States was long and tiring. I assumed the plane would fly straight through to the East Coast, but again, no. None of us knew we would be spending the night in Ohio. We arrived at a base—I think it was an air force base—and we waited our turn to be taken from the gigantic plane into a rest area for the night. As I was carried from the plane, I could hear what sounded like a thousand voices screaming at the top of their lungs. Maybe it was a welcome home gathering for us, but in that short distance to the rest area, all we could hear were protesters calling us every name in the book. Thank God we were separated by a fence. These people were so angry and so determined to disrupt our passage. Once inside the building, we could still hear, hour after hour, the threats and the disgusting language. *Who are these people?* I wondered. I guess I expected at least a slight welcome home, but these protesters were intent on making their voices heard.

I tried to somehow justify to myself that I played a small role in assuring their right to protest, but it was still hard to swallow. These people had no respect even for those who had died, much less for those who would be disabled for the rest of their lives. "Forget it, Gordon," I told myself. "Some day they will look at us in a different light."

As the sun rose the next morning, I awakened to the loud and ugly voices of the protesters. They were the same ones who gave us such a "warm welcome" the day before. I suppose they wanted to give us a meaningful send-off as well. Loaded onto the C-141, I thought, *I'm getting closer to home.* I remember some of the flight crew encouraging us to hold on, it wouldn't be long now. Because I was given pain medicine before we taxied to the runway, I fell asleep quickly. I woke up a couple of hours into the flight to hear the screams of pain from some of my comrades. I lay still and was thankful my wounds weren't as serious as some of theirs. One hour out from Andrews Air Force Base, I began to be excited. Now I knew for sure that I would make it home. Even though that home for the next eighteen months would be DeWitt Army Hospital at Ft. Belvoir, Virginia, I was still content.

The next thing I knew, I was off the plane and loaded into an air force van for the short trip to DeWitt. I was so excited to think I was almost there. I had waited for this day for what seemed like an eternity. I would soon be reunited with my wife, Joy! As the van entered the emergency room entrance, I saw her. She was more beautiful than when I left her eleven months ago. Finally, I was where I had wanted to be for so many months—in her arms, hugging her with all my strength, which at that point wasn't much. I just wanted to hold her forever. I felt so safe in her arms. Preparing for the transfer to my room, I noted the windows of the hospital were filled with smiling faces. An audience of encouragers had enjoyed our reunion as much as we did almost!

# Chapter 13

## My Friend Ron

While most of my treatment was taken care of at Ft. Belvoir, I did have an occasion to visit the hand clinic at Walter Reed Army Hospital in Washington DC. I had no idea that on my first visit there I would be reunited with a friend who was wounded a few months before I was. The memories flooded back vividly, as if it were yesterday.

It was a warm, windy day on the South China Sea, kind of a stand-down, if you will. I remember the hooches (shelters) and the Vietnamese people as they continued to go about their daily lives, though they were surrounded by a company of American soldiers. The day was beautiful, with a clear blue sky, and for one day, the smell of firefights was nowhere in the air. The day went smoothly. We were laid-back, enjoying the stiff breeze that blew off the water. About 4 o'clock, I heard the familiar barking of the first sergeant, "Saddle up," meaning, "Get your gear on, lock and load, and let's get back to war." It was strangely great; from unusual bliss back to our purpose in Vietnam in the first place: kill all the enemy we could. When ready, we moved out and headed away from the sand and back into the jungles, that place we knew so well and had earned our greatest respect. At the head of our column walked a young radio operator named Ron, whom I had gotten to know very well. In fact, we had spoken earlier that morning. Ron had seven days left; only seven days and then away from the stench of Vietnam. Even though I wished it were me, I was happy for Ron. He had plans to be married on his return home. We could not have known that those plans, the happiness that Ron was feeling, were to be cut short. His plans and his life were soon to be changed forever.

As the column cleared the beach, the familiar result of an explosion shook the ground. Dear God, what now? As we picked ourselves up off the sand, the talk made its way to us. Someone set off a booby trap. The Vietnamese had wired a 175 artillery round. All that was left to do was for someone to trip the wire. The victim: Ron. I raced ahead and found Ron on the sand, with both legs gone and medics working feverishly to save his life. My anguished thoughts were, *Why Ron? He's supposed to go home in seven days.* His plans—gone. Life as he knew it—over. I could only shake my head as Ron screamed and writhed in pain. The medics did a phenomenal job controlling his bleeding with tourniquets and administering morphine for pain. Shortly, the Medivac helicopter circled overhead, moved in quickly, and Ron was scooped up from the area. I did not know that Ron and I would reunite many months later. I thought about Ron nearly every day and how that booby trap had drastically and awfully changed his life.

In early 1969, I was supposed to have an appointment with a hand surgeon in Walter Reed Army Hospital. How massive the place was! As I searched for the right office, I mistakenly entered a ward that treated traumatic brain injuries. I could not believe the horror I witnessed. Kids, a ward of kids who could not speak, being fed intravenously, and with no movement in their bodies. My own injuries felt of no consequence compared to my fellow soldiers on that ward. I left the ward sick to my stomach, thinking, *Their lives are gone.* I wondered how the families must feel, knowing their loved ones would be confined to a wheelchair for the rest of their life. *Some,* I thought, *might never even leave this hospital.* This war had taken its toll on thousands of soldiers and their families. I remember thinking, *I wish I could help in some way, but how could I, a man also recuperating from the effects of war.*

On exiting the ward, I found a chair, sat down, and buried my head in my hands. I just could not get that nightmarish scene out of my mind. Composing myself, I took up my search again for the hand clinic. As I walked along the halls, I saw in the distance a wheelchair coming at warp speed! The chair and the person in it passed me so quickly I could barely see him. Suddenly, as I looked back, the chair stopped and turned around, heading back toward me. Ron! It was Ron! The last time I saw Ron he was near death, and now he was there with me at the army hospital. We hugged for a moment and then shared memories of the day he was injured so badly. I was so glad to see him. *He looks good,* I thought, and it was then I realized that Ron would be okay. I still had to find the hand clinic, but now I had a buddy rolling beside me in his wheelchair, helping me. We said our good-byes and off he rolled down the hallway of Walter Reed Hospital. What a day it had been: an emotional roller coaster that began by accidentally straying off to the wrong ward only to be reunited with Ron. God was still working miracles in my life.

I left Walter Reed with mixed emotions, so happy for Ron but overwhelmed by the traumatic brain injury ward. I have never forgotten that day, and I probably never will. Yet, I consider that day one of the blessings in my life. Each time I visit the VA hospital, even now, the memories all come back. Many suffer to this day from the war in Vietnam. I only wish people would find it in their hearts to visit these injured, lonesome men confined in a place they will never leave.

# Chapter 14

## Finally, Going Home

I got good news that day at the hand clinic. Just one more operation on my left arm and then I could go home, my real home, for some R&R. I thought, "Man, I can't wait." It felt like an eternity since I left the small apartment Joy and I called home. We had so many happy moments there before I received my draft notice. I was going back … back to where we had started our life together … back to some sort of normal living.

About a week later, operation over, I was headed east on Interstate 64. Even the road looked beautiful to me. Three hours later and there it was, our apartment. It was just as I remembered, just as I left it when I was on top of the world. After a few days at home, I received more bad news. My friend Ricky Huggett, with whom I went to high school, was killed in Vietnam. I thought I would be able to put this war to rest, but with the news of Ricky's death, my mind once again drifted toward Southeast Asia. I remember trying to summon enough nerve to visit Ricky's parents, people I had known all my life. When my eyes met theirs, I lost it, as did they. They were so happy that I was home and safe. For just a moment, they lifted my spirits and then came a wave of intense grief. I had to go. It was just too much for one day. I was emotionally crushed. I still think of Ricky, a life ended much too soon. I will see you again, my friend.

I eventually did begin to relax and enjoyed being home with my bride. But as in the past, more sorrow would come in just a few short weeks. Gilbert Page, another high school friend, died in the battle for Hamburger Hill. *Dear God, when will it be over?* I wondered, *When will all the sorrow and grief stop? How many more young men and women must die before someone realizes that it's time to stop?* It finally did stop after fifty-eight thousand deaths and hundreds of thousands wounded. But it *did* stop.

Joy and I somehow made it through the funerals for Gilbert and Ricky. As "Taps" was played in the distance at each funeral, we felt the tears run down our faces. We looked over each casket covered with the US flag, and saw the families of these soldiers totally destroyed. "Dear God, comfort them. They need you as much as I needed you on that mountain trail."

# Chapter 15

## It's Over—Now What

Finally, I was going to be medically retired from the US Army. The doctors did all they could to renew the use of my left arm and hand. My injuries pale in comparison to thousands of wounded soldiers who will never be mobile again. As I think about it, I am so blessed to have lived.

I fast-forward several years. Our first son, Scott, was born. It is hard to believe that he has now turned forty years old. Three years after Scott's birth came another blessed day. Our second son, Brian, joined our family. I remember thinking they were so innocent, with no knowledge of war and how evil it can be. It has only been in the last four years that I have been able to share my story with them. In fact, telling them about my experience really prompted my memory of my promise to God. I promised God to tell everyone what He did for me on February 27, 1968. God has continued to bless me and my family. Not a day goes by that I am not grateful beyond words.

There have still been challenges. Just when I thought I had left the memories of Vietnam behind, the doctors told me I had prostate cancer. How could that be? I was devastated. Soon, I learned that this cancer could be the result of stomping through areas in Vietnam that had been sprayed with a defoliant known as Agent Orange. That little country in Southeast Asia, some thirteen thousand miles away, had struck again. Once again, God spared my life. It has been eight years since I had prostate cancer, and all is well. What a blessed man I am.

Shortly after being retired medically from the military, I tried my hand at banking. Somehow I just wasn't happy doing that kind of work. I knew I had to work, but felt I was not suited for this type of employment. I remember starting to spiral downward because my future was unsettled, but again God showed up when I least expected Him. A neighbor asked if I was interested in being in business for myself. He and his brother had operated a box and barrel company which supplied seafood containers to the seafood industry for many years and now both brothers wanted to retire. I sought the advice of my dear friend, Jimmy Gray Forrest. Jimmy, being a banker and also being an accountant and doing the tax returns for that particular business for many years, thought it would be a good move for me if I could secure the funds to purchase the company. After long talks with Joy, we decided to take the risk. A small business loan was approved and we found ourselves in business not knowing what the future had in store for us.

My first year in business found the James River and many of its tributaries frozen solid. The fishing boats along with the oyster and crab boats found themselves out of work due to the severe weather. I thought to myself, I'll be bankrupted shortly! What on earth am I going to do? And then it hit me, I'll pray and I prayed all of the time about this situation. Slowly the weather improved and sales began to flourish. For thirty five years, God blessed that business and continues to cause it to grow and provide for my two sons and their families who are the new owners.

As I think back now, God had a plan for my life and my experiences in Southeast Asia were just a part of that plan. I see life more clearly now as if my eyes had blinders that have now been removed. I see the poor and the helpless differently than before Vietnam. I witnessed firsthand the undeserving, awful treatment that was forced on the South Vietnamese people. They were just ordinary families wanting only to be left alone so they could raise their children. Wanting to plant and reap their meager gardens and try to enjoy their lives while being threatened daily with bombs and bullets.

The poor and desperate, in our country, need our assistance in so many ways. It took Vietnam to make me see I had a duty to those who are less fortunate than me. It's difficult to explain how war can change a person. I entered Vietnam a 19 year old kid and returned a man with a purpose. While I have faltered and yes fallen, God continued to supply everything I needed to make a difference in my family and community.

I recall my very first attempt at public service. I joined the local volunteer fire department and enjoyed every aspect of the job. Over the years as a volunteer, I was privileged to hold many offices. You can only imagine the exhilaration I felt when I was elected by my peers to become their chief. I was honored and so proud to be able to assist my fellow citizens trying to protect them from the ravages of fire and emergency situations. Some years later, for whatever reason, I decided that I could better assist my fellow citizens if I could be elected to city council. I chewed on that possibility for months. Then God showed up again with just the push I needed. I ran for a seat on city council and was elected. After an evening of celebration, I remember thinking; what have you done? I guess you could say; I jumped out of the frying pan into the fire. It was difficult giving up the volunteer company and the remarkable service we all provided. I was proud to be a part of that department and served as their chief for eight years, however, I believed I was clearly being led to serve in another capacity.

From 1982 until 2010, I served my community as a Council Member, Vice Mayor and lastly Mayor. For 28 years, I poured my life into my community. If I was successful, then to God, my family and the city staff be the glory.

In 2010 another thought entered my mind; serving my community and my state made a lot of sense to me. I guess you could say I felt led to run for a state office. I ran for a seat in the Virginia State House of Delegates and was elected. I proudly serve there today. I do not know how long my run in the Legislature will be, but God does and I know at some point in time He will show up and make it clear what my next move will be. Until then, I will pray for His continued blessings and guidance.

Before ending the words of this book, I must thank God for the prosperity He has provided me and my family. I must thank my wife, Joy and my sons Scott and Brian for sharing their husband and father with each task I became involved in. To my many friends who have always been there to help me through long difficult times, I am forever grateful.

My story, my ordeal, is not unlike that of many others. Like others, I have learned many great lessons from my experiences. I discovered that before Vietnam, I was traveling a road that had no end and really no purpose. I realized that God had a much higher calling for me, and I now truly try to do those things that God would want me to do. I try to do things daily that will bring a smile to His face. I realize I have a long way to go with regard to my walk with God. I am also hopeful that this book will in some way touch another that may be drifting, as I was, and that it might encourage others to share their stories. I pray my words have somehow convinced someone that no matter how high the mountain or how low the valley, when you feel you can't go on, God will show up!

Some forty-five years ago, on a mountain trail, God showed up to save me. Call on God. Trust in God. God will show up for you, too.

Christmas Eve 1967 (Gordon on right)

Christmas Day 1967 (Gordon third from right, behind tree)

**Break from search and destroy mission,
January 1968 (Gordon)**

**Resupply Helicopter (Gordon)**